Moments with God for Children

Prayers for Little Ones

BARBARA YOUNGER

DIMENSIONS
FOR LIVING
NASHVILLE

A Moment with God for Children:
Prayers for Little Ones

This book is printed on acid-free, recycled paper.

Library of Congress Cataloging-in-Publication Data

Younger, Barbara, 1954–
A moment with God for children : prayers for little ones/Barbara Younger.
p. c.m.
Summary: Provides fifty-eight brief prayers, each accompanied by a Scripture reading.
ISBN 0-687-12205-8 (pbk. : alk. paper)
1. Children—Prayer-books and devotions—English.
[1. Prayer books and devotions.] I. Title.
BV265.Y68 1997
242'.62—dc21 97-14989

97 98 99 00 01 02 03 04 05 06—10 9 8 7 6 5 4 3 2

MANUFACTURED IN THE UNITED STATES OF AMERICA

CONTENTS

THE ALPHABET

"I am the first and the last, the beginning and the end." —*Revelation 22:13*

Dear God,

Listen to me as I say my ABC's:
A-B-C-D-E-F-G
H-I-J-K-L-M-N-O-P
Q-R-S, T-U-V
W-X and Y and Z!
Thank you for letters that become words.
Thank you for words that become stories
and poems and prayers.
Amen.

AMAZING THINGS

"At God's command amazing things happen, wonderful things that we can't understand." —*Job 37:5*

Dear God,

I can't always explain
the amazing things that happen.
Why does my dog love me so much?
Why does watermelon taste delicious?
Why do I like to dance to my favorite songs?
Why do babies wiggle their toes?
Why does my grandpa make such funny jokes?
Even though I don't understand,
I thank you, God,
for the amazing things that happen
over and over again.
Amen.

ARGUING

Don't argue with someone for no reason
when he has never done you any harm.
—Proverbs 3:30

Dear God,

Sometimes my sister and I
argue for no reason.
Sometimes, I think, we argue
just for something to do.
Help us find better ways
to spend our days:
homemade boats that proudly float;
mud cakes that take hours to bake;
cardboard cars for pretend movie stars;
or fairylands made of sticks and sand.
Amen.

BABIES

She put the baby in it and then placed it in the tall grass at the edge of the river.
—*Exodus 2:3*b

Dear God,

If I found Baby Moses in the river grass,
I would bring him home
and rock him and sing to him
and teach him games like pat-a-cake.
I'm glad you made babies, God,
for big kids like me to entertain.
Amen.

BIBLE STORIES

Write down for the coming generation
what the LORD has done,
so that people not yet born will
praise him.

—Psalm 102:18

Dear God,

Adam and Eve,
Jonah and the whale,
Noah and his ark,
Mary and Martha,
Zaccheaus in the tree,
and the boy with loaves and fishes:
Hooray for stories that show
the faith of Bible people
who lived long, long ago!
Amen.

BOOKS

He had a small scroll open in his hand.
—Revelation 10:2

Dear God,

Children in Bible times didn't have
books to read as we do today.
Thanks for big books and little books,
picture books and books with lots of
words,
sad books and funny books,
pop-up books and talking books.
I bet Bible kids would have
enjoyed the books I like to read!
Amen.

BUTTERFLIES AND EASTER

They found the stone rolled away from the entrance to the tomb. —*Luke 24:2*

Dear God,

As the caterpillar leaves the cocoon,
born anew as a butterfly,
Jesus came out of the tomb
as our Risen Lord.
Whenever I see a butterfly, I remember
the wonderful story of Easter morning.
Amen.

CHEERFUL GIVING

Each one should give, then, as he has decided, not with regret or out of a sense of duty; for God loves the one who gives gladly.
—2 Corinthians 9:7

Dear God,

When I was in the store, picking out the present, I was happy.
When I wrapped it, I was happy with my gift.
As I left for the birthday party,
I just knew my friend would love what I had chosen.
But at the party, when I gave the present,
I really wanted to keep it for myself.
I hated to give it up.
Please God, help me to be a cheerful giver.
Amen.

CLOUDS

"Do you know how clouds float in the sky,
the work of God's amazing skill?"
—Job 37:16

Dear God,

I think you are clever to make clouds float in the sky.
I like to lie on my back and decide what shapes they make:
an elephant, a tree, a frog,
a bicycle, a baseball cap,
and a cupcake with
marshmallow frosting.
Amen.

COUNTING

"Even the hairs of your head have all been counted." —*Luke 12:7*

Dear God,

One banana,
Two cousins,
Three caterpillars,
Four leaves,
Five frogs:
I'm glad you made so many wonderful things for me to count.
Hooray for numbers!
Amen.

FLYING

"All the wild birds are mine
and all living things in the field."
—Psalm 50:11

Dear God,

Every now and then I pretend to fly;
the birds make it look so easy!
Since I'm a child and don't have wings or feathers,
I guess I won't be flying without the help of a plane.
Still, God, I'm glad you made birds that fly.
They look like they're having fun, soaring above the earth,
and I have fun watching them from my spot on the ground. Amen.

FOREVER GOD

Before you created the hills
or brought the world into being,
you were eternally God,
and will be God forever.
—Psalm 90:2

Dear God,

Bubbles burst,
balloons pop,
ice melts, and even
flowers don't last forever.
But the Bible tells me
that you are forever,
and that you always
will be my God.
Amen.

FORGIVING OTHERS

Be kind and tender-hearted to one another, and forgive one another, as God has forgiven you through Christ.

—Ephesians 4:32

Dear God,

Today,
one friend pushed me, another pinched.
My brother teased me and wouldn't
let me touch any of his toys.
And to top it all off,
my mother made me clean up
my room, when it wasn't even messy!
Help me to forgive all of them.
Amen.

A GENTLE ANSWER

A gentle answer quiets anger, but a harsh one stirs it up. —*Proverbs 15:1*

Dear God,

Yesterday,
when my friend and I were playing,
she said something mean.
I was so mad that I almost shouted back.
But I didn't.
And you know what, God?
The rest of the day we got along great!
Amen.

GOD MADE THE WORLD

God looked at everything he had made, and he was very pleased. —*Genesis 1:31*

Dear God,

I'm not at all surprised that
you were pleased when
you finished creating the world.
I'd be pleased, too, if I could make
a world like ours!
Amen.

GOOD DEEDS

[E]ncourage you and strengthen you to always do and say what is good.
—2 Thessalonians 2:17

Dear God,

This is going to be a week of good deeds:
Sunday, I'll write a letter to Grandma.
Monday, I'll take out the trash.
Tuesday, I'll play house with my cat.
Wednesday, I'll draw a picture for my teacher.
Thursday, I'll visit a neighbor who is lonely.
Friday, I'll sort a huge pile of socks.
Saturday, I'll help cook supper.
And when this week is through,
I might think of more good deeds to do.
Amen.

THE GOOD SAMARITAN

But a Samaritan who was traveling that way came upon the man, and when he saw him, his heart was filled with pity.

—Luke 10:33

Dear God,

All my life,
may I be like
the good Samaritan,
ready to help
anyone who needs me.
Amen.

THE GOOD SHEPHERD

"I am the good shepherd. As the Father knows me and I know the Father, in the same way I know my sheep and they know me."
—John 10:14

Dear God,

Just as good shepherds care
for all their sheep,
I know that Jesus cares
for all the people
in his flock,
including me!
Amen.

GROWN-UPS

Their instructions are a shining light; their correction can teach you how to live.
—Proverbs 6:23

Dear God,

Sometimes I get tired of
grown-ups telling me
how to behave,
but I know that
grown-ups
are part of your plan
for helping us kids
grow up!
Amen.

HELPING OTHERS

"The King will reply, 'tell you, whenever you did this for one of the least important of these brothers of mine, you did it for me!' "
—Matthew 25:40

Dear God,

May I always be aware
That there are people everywhere
Who need food and clothes
And homes and medicine
And lots of extra care.
Amen.

HIDE AND SEEK

"Ask, and you will receive; seek and you will find; knock, and the door will be opened to you."
—Matthew 7:7

Dear God,

Hide and Seek
Is one of my favorite games.
I almost always think
of great hiding places.
But I'm glad, God, that
no matter where I hide,
you can always find me.
Amen.

THE HOLY SPIRIT

"I will ask the Father, and he will give you another Helper, who will stay with you forever." *—John 14:16*

Dear God,

Sometimes I'm brave.
Remember how high I went on the ferris wheel?
But other times, I'm afraid.
Remember how I cried when I got lost at the fair?
But I know that, brave or afraid,
you are always with me.
Even though I can't see you,
I know that your Holy Spirit
is always by my side.
Amen.

ICE-CREAM SUNDAE

"This is how he feeds the people
and provides an abundance of food."
—Job 36:31

Dear God,

Vanilla ice cream, hot fudge,
whipped cream, caramel sauce,
nuts, sprinkles, and a cherry on top!
This delicious sundae reminds me
that you have blessed us
with lots of good food.
Amen.

I'M SORRY

"If we say that we have no sin, we deceive ourselves, and there is no truth in us."

—1 John 1:8

Dear God,

I know that sometimes
I do things that you
don't want me to do.
But I am a child who is
willing to say, "I'm sorry."
And you are a God who forgives.
Amen.

IN OUR HEARTS

"They look on the outward appearance, but the LORD looks on the heart."
*—1 Samuel 16:7*c *NRSV*

Dear God,

When I'm having fun cutting out paper hearts,
it doesn't bother me if they are crooked.
You don't care if we look perfect either, God,
because you don't look at our outward appearance.
You look for the goodness in our hearts.
Amen.

JESUS CALLED THE CHILDREN

But Jesus called the children to him and said, "Let the children come to me and do not stop them, because the Kingdom of God belongs to such as these."

—Luke 18:16

Dear God,

I'm glad the children in the Bible
were able to visit with Jesus.
It's good to know that he thought
children are important.
Amen.

LEARNING TO WRITE

See what big letters I make as I write to you now with my own hand!

—Galatians 6:11

Dear God,

I'm glad I'm learning to write.
Now I can print words:
LOVE, HELLO, THANK YOU—
words that are perfect for a letter
to my grandma or to a friend who is sick.
And when I get to the end of my letter,
I can even sign my very own name!
Amen.

LOVE ONE ANOTHER

"And now I give you a new commandment: love one another. As I have loved you, so you must love one another." —*John 13:34*

Dear God,

You sent Jesus from above
to show the world how to love.
And now kids like me
can help other kids to see
how to love one another.
Amen.

MAKE ME A PEACEMAKER

"Happy are those who work for peace;
God will call them his children!"
—Matthew 5:9

Dear God,

Even kids can work for peace
by speaking to a mean classmate,
waving to a grumpy neighbor,
helping fix a broken toy,
smiling at a frowning brother or sister,
making breakfast for a tired mother.
Kids can work for peace in lots of ways.
Make me a peacemaker every day.
Amen.

MERRY CHRISTMAS

She gave birth to her first son, wrapped him in cloths and laid him in a manger—there was no room for them to stay in the inn.
—Luke 2:7

Dear God,

With carols and cookies,
Trees and tinsel,
Pageants, lights, and presents,
We celebrate once again
the birth of your Son, Jesus.
Merry Christmas!
Amen.

THE MOON

So God made the two larger lights, the sun to rule over the day and the moon to rule over the night. —*Genesis 1:16*a

Dear God,

There's a Mother Goose rhyme that goes:
 I see the moon and the moon sees me,
 God bless the moon and God bless me.
I'm not certain that the moon sees me,
but I know that you see me, God.
Thanks for watching me as I sleep at night.
And thanks for the moon that I like to watch
from my bedroom window,
just before I go to sleep.
Amen.

MY BED

When I lie down, I go to sleep in peace.
—Psalm 4:8

Dear God,

My very own bed
is one of my favorite places
in the whole wide world.
It makes me sad to think
that some children don't have
warm and comfortable beds.
I pray that one day
children everywhere
will have beds like mine
to call their own.
Amen.

MY BIRTHDAY

I have relied on you since the day I was born,
and you have always been my God.
—Psalm 22:10

Dear God,

I'm learning about the calendar
and the days and months in the year.
Watch me point to an important date,
a day for which I can hardly wait:
My birthday!
Thanks for giving me
a day to celebrate ME.
Amen.

NAMES

Israel, the LORD who created you says,
"Do not be afraid—I will save you.
I have called you by name—you are mine."
—Isaiah 43:1

Dear God,

So many people,
with all sorts of names:
Hannah, Michael, and Shane,
Joshua, Carlos, and Kate,
Yumiko, Lauren, and Tate,
Tonya, Nicholas, and Beth,
Ryan, Sarah, and Seth,
Maria, Lea, and Paul.
The Bible says you know them all.
You must have a super memory, God!
Amen.

NOAH'S ARK

"Build a boat for yourself out of good timber; make rooms in it and cover it with tar inside and out." —*Genesis 6:14*

Dear God,

I like to pretend that my bed is a boat
and that I am Noah.
I bring aboard all my animals,
and together we sail on the water.
Thanks for letting Noah
save the animals,
And thanks for all the animals
that Noah saved.
Amen.

PATHS

He guides me in the right paths,
as he has promised.
—Psalm 23:3

Dear God,

I like to follow a path.
Paths help me know the best way to go.
As I grow up and grow in faith, I pray
that you lead me down the right paths.
Amen.

PATIENCE

"I know what you have done; I know how hard you have worked and how patient you have been." —*Revelation 2:2*

Dear God,

My yo-yo string is terribly tangled;
I'm having trouble learning to ride
my two-wheeler;
I can't tie my shoelaces;
and my block tower just fell over.
"Patience!" my mother says.
"Take your time!" my father calls.
God, it's hard for kids to be patient.
I'm glad you understand.
Amen.

PLANTS

So the earth produced all kinds of plants,
and God was pleased with what he saw.
—Genesis 1:12

Dear God,

What a splendid artist
you must be!
The earth is decorated
with plants
of every size,
and shape,
and color.
Amen.

PRAISING GOD

Then he went into the Temple with them,
walking and jumping and praising God.
—*Acts 3:8*b

Dear God,

I'm not sure
that my parents
will let me
jump in church,
but maybe next week
I could take a giant leap
just before I walk
through the door,
just to show everyone
how happy I am
to come to your house.
Amen.

PRAYER

Pray at all times. —*1 Thessalonians 5:17*

Dear God,

I can pray to you
Anytime,
Anywhere,
About anything at all.
Now that's cool!
Amen.

PRAYING FOR OTHERS

"We always thank God for you all and always mention you in our prayers."
—1 Thessalonians 1:2

Dear God,

Bless all the people I love.
I will say their names now as I pray. . . .
Amen.

PRESENTS

They went into the house, and when they saw the child with his mother Mary, they knelt down and worshiped him. They brought out their gifts of gold, frankincense, and myrrh, and presented them to him.
—Matthew 2:11

Dear God,

If I were going to visit
Baby Jesus, I might bring:
A picture I drew,
A collage I created,
A pie I helped to make,
Or a poem I wrote.
Presents don't need to be fancy
like those the wise men brought.
But I know that
presents should show
plenty of thought!
Amen.

A PROMISE

He will keep his covenant forever,
his promises for a thousand generations.
—Psalm 105:8

Dear God,

I promise
to remember
your promise
to love me
forever.
Amen.

PUMPKINS

"Celebrate the Harvest Festival when you begin to harvest your crops."

—Exodus 23:16

Dear God,

Thanks for making
Small seeds
that grow,
and grow,
and grow,
and grow
Into enormous pumpkins!
Amen.

QUESTIONS, QUESTIONS

On the third day they found him in the Temple, sitting with the Jewish teachers, listening to them and asking questions.

—Luke 2:46

Dear God,

Every now and then my parents say,
"You're asking too many questions.
It's time to go to bed."
But I know they don't really mind,
because kids should ask questions,
just as Jesus did when he was a boy.
Help me to ask the questions I need to ask,
and to listen carefully to the answers.
Amen.

RAIN

You caused abundant rain to fall
and restored your worn-out land.
—Psalm 68:9

Dear God,

Rain, I think, was a good idea.
I like to hear the rain on the roof;
I like to remember the plants
that need a fresh drink;
I like to picture the ponds and lakes
filling up again;
But most of all,
I like to splash in the puddles!
Amen.

RAINBOW COLORS

"I am putting my bow in the clouds. It will be the sign of my covenant with the world."
—Genesis 9:13

Dear God,

With my paints,
I just created
a spectacular rainbow—
Red, Orange, Yellow,
Green, Blue, and Purple.
I'll hang it on my door
for everyone to admire,
as a rainbow reminder
that you have painted
our world with color.
Amen.

REST

He lets me rest in fields of green grass
and leads me to quiet pools of fresh water.
—Psalm 23:2

Dear God,

Taking a rest
in green grass
on a warm summer day
seems like
a bit of heaven
on earth.
Amen.

SEA CREATURES

So God created the great sea monsters, all kinds of creatures that live in the water, and all kinds of birds. And God was pleased with what he saw. —*Genesis 1:21*

Dear God,

You must have had
the best time filling
the oceans with creatures:
Stingrays and Loggerhead Turtles,
Starfish, Batfish, Angelfish,
Sharks, Eels, Squids, Dolphins,
and the biggest sea creature of all,
the magnificent blue Whale.
Amen.

SINGING

Sing a new song to the Lord!
Sing to the Lord, all the world!
—Psalm 96:1

Dear God,

I like to make up
brand new songs
and sing them just for you.
What a fun way to pray!
Amen.

THE STARS

"Can you guide the stars season by season and direct the Big and the Little Dipper?"
—Job 38:32

Dear God,

On starry nights, I'm learning
to find the Big Dipper and the Little Dipper.
When you set the stars in the sky, God,
I'm glad you made such neat shapes!
Amen.

STEPS

"God knows everything I do;
he sees every step I take."
—Job 31:4

Dear God,

One step, two steps,
Third steps, four,
Five, and six,
Watch me take some more.
Seven steps, eight steps,
Nine and ten.
And now it's time to say
Amen.

TEACHERS

Keep my teaching with you all the time;
write it on your heart. —*Proverbs 7:3*

Dear God,

Thank you for teachers
who spend their days
teaching kids like me.
Tomorrow, I think
I'll thank *my* teacher.
Amen.

TEARS

Jesus wept. —*John 11:35*

Dear God,

The Bible tells me
that sometimes Jesus cried.
That makes me feel better,
because sometimes I cry, too.
Amen.

TEMPERS

Hot tempers cause arguments, but patience brings peace. —*Proverbs 15:18*

Dear God,

Whenever I get really mad,
I am glad that
You are there
to remind me
that patience brings peace.
Amen.

THANK YOU, LORD!

I will always thank the LORD;
I will never stop praising him.
—Psalm 34:1

Dear God,

Morning, noon, and night,
I praise you with all my might.
Thank you,
Thank you,
Thank you,
Lord!
Amen.

WASHING

Then he poured some water into a washbasin and began to wash the disciples' feet and dry them with the towel around his waist.
—John 13:5

Dear God,

Grown-ups always worry
about kids getting clean.
The Bible says that Jesus
washed the feet of his disciples.
I guess that even in Bible times,
grown-ups liked to wash.
Maybe when I'm a grown-up,
I will too.
Amen.

THE WIND AND GOD

"The wind blows wherever it wishes; you hear the sound it makes, but you do not know where it comes from or where it is going."
—John 3:8

Dear God,

Even though I can't see it,
I know the wind is there.
I hear the sound it makes
as it whips through the trees.
I can't see you either, God,
but I know you are there.
I hear sounds of you all around me:
Crickets chirping, birds singing,
Streams bubbling, frogs croaking,
And the voices of the people I love.
Amen.